cover these pages with a collage of memories from your

Crayons, colored pencils and double stick tape work great for this book!

First published by Jennifer Tookoian in 2014

Jennifer Tookoian
2037 W. Bullard #165
Fresno, CA 93711

www.itsallgoodbooks.com

978-0-9916461-3-5

vacation. Use pictures, postcards or anything you like.

Color this!

NAME

DATE

Created by Jennie Tookoian
Designed & Illustrated by Elisabeth Markus

How this Memory Book Works

This is your book of memories. Be creative and make it your own. Don't worry about going in order - hop around from page to page. If you don't like a topic on the page, cross it out and change it, glue pictures over it or even tear it out and throw it away.

You can sketch your ideas or use a digital camera to snap your photos and glue them to your memory book. Find interesting things like shells, postcards or other things from your trip and glue them too. Print your pictures at your hotel while you are on vacation, or when you get home.

What you will need: a camera (if you want), pencils, markers, glue sticks, maybe scissors and your imagination.

Take advantage of the local resources. This means grab brochures, find postcards, things from the beach or in the hotel. Talk to the people who work there or live in Palm Beach. Cut out things you like and glue them into your book.

Make friends with the people around you. Have fun and make some memories.

We promise you, if you have fun with this and record your memories, you will have a great time reading it in 1, 5, or even 10 or more years from now. Enjoy!

This vacation **Memory Book** was created by

_____

What's the date of your trip?

How old are you?

Which cities are you traveling to or through?

Why are you going there?

Take a picture or sketch yourself from the beginning of your vacation... glue it here

3

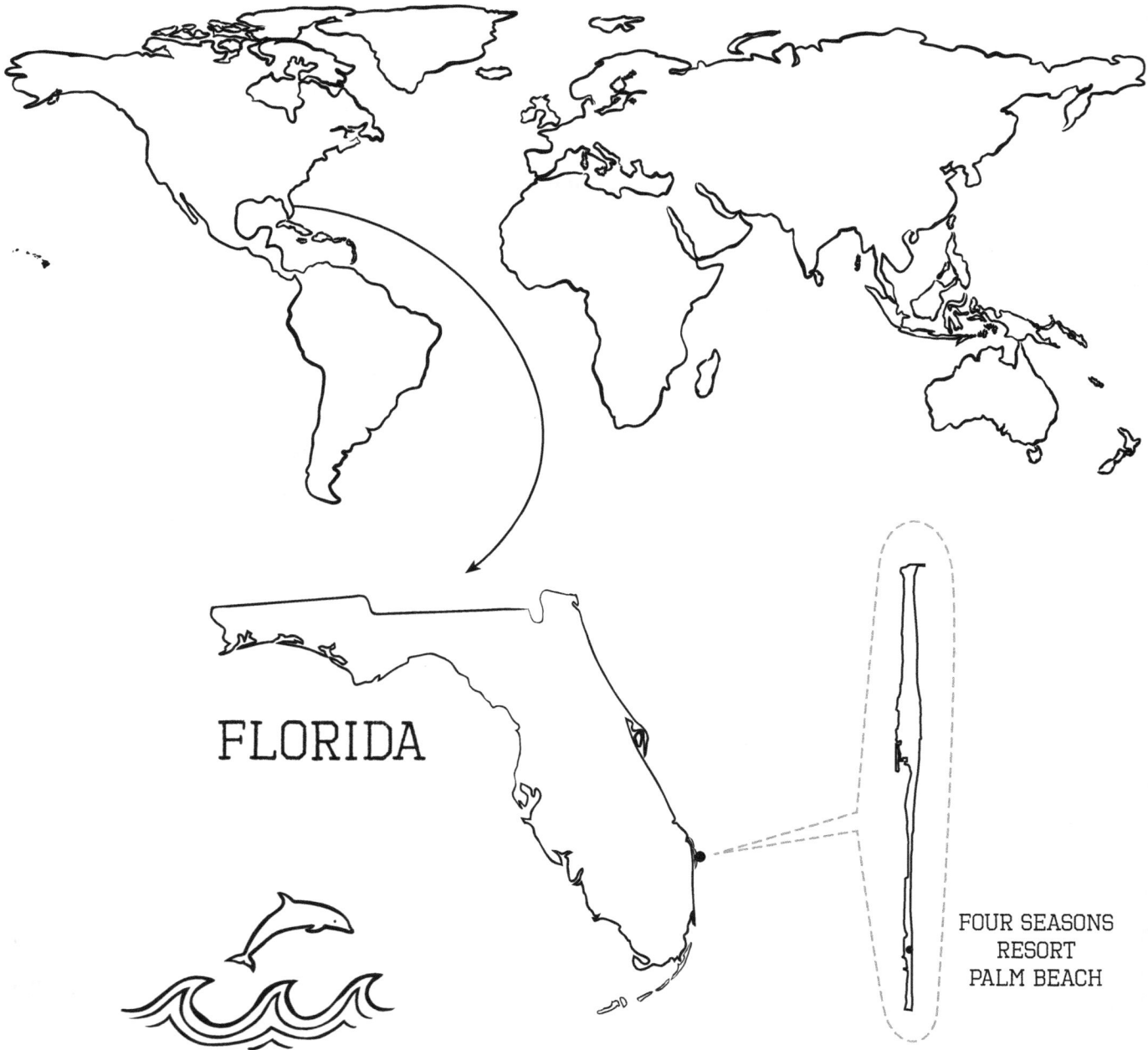

Locate your trip on a **Global Map**. Draw a line from your home to your vacation spot. **Color** the map, use **stickers** or a *SYMBOL* like a ☆ to show your home and your vacation spot.

FLORIDA

FOUR SEASONS
RESORT
PALM BEACH

My first hour in Palm Beach...

The weather is:

It feels like:

I hear:

I smell:

I see :

The first thing I want to do is ...

The first thing I see in Palm Beach that I don't have at home is...

5

Take a photo or draw a **picture** of the view
from your hotel/bedroom window
(OR FIND A COOL PLACE IF YOU'VE GOT A CRUDDY VIEW... HEY, IT HAPPENS!)

Collect 6 things from the **ocean**, the **beach** or nature that are smaller than your palm. Photograph and/or glue them to this page.
MAKE SURE NOT TO TAKE ANYTHING FROM PROTECTED AREAS SUCH AS STATE PARKS OR TIDAL POOLS.

1

2

3

4

5

6

Find a good place to watch the sunset. Take a **photograph** or SKETCH the sunset for a few days. Sketch or paste them here. *JOT DOWN THE DIFFERENCES BETWEEN THE DAYS.*

DAY 1

DAY 2

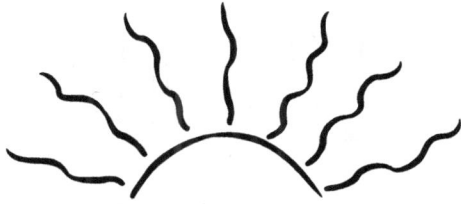

#1

#2

#3

The best one was...

LET'S EAT!!

1st Meal

where?   when?

rate it!

last Meal

where?   when?

Best Meal

where?   when?

Scavenger Hunt

RACE AGAINST A FRIEND TO FIND ALL OF THESE ITEMS, OR SET A GOAL FOR HOW LONG IT WILL TAKE YOU AND RACE AGAINST THE CLOCK TO BEAT YOUR TIME.

- [ ] someone crossing the street and looking at their cell phone
- [ ] an interesting person on the beach — create a story about them (you can use the pages in the back)
- [ ] a baby sleeping
- [ ] someone with a sunburn
- [ ] Someone dancing
- [ ] two people wearing the same bathing suit
- [ ] a shell that looks like an animal
- [ ] somebody playing a drum
- [ ] someone speaking another language
- [ ] someone humming or singing too loudly
- [ ] someone drinking a drink that has something in it (umbrella, flower, pineapple)
- [ ] an animal bigger than your hand
- [ ] a grown man eating ice cream
- [ ] someone with a moustache
- [ ] a bratty kid
- [ ] a set of twins
- [ ] find an annoying person and make them smile
- [ ] a sand castle
- [ ] a piece of coral
- [ ] someone with a flower in their hair
- [ ] a catamaran
- [ ] someone wearing a flower shirt
- [ ] a tropical plant that is taller than you
- [ ] eat a tropical fruit
- [ ] someone wearing a ridiculous hat
- [ ] someone surfing
- [ ] a family playing on the beach

GLUE A BORDER ON THIS PAGE WITH
INTERESTING THINGS FROM YOUR TRIP
{SAND, SHELLS, WRAPPERS, LINT — ?!?}
GLUE A PICTURE OR A BUNCH OF PICTURES OF YOU
ON YOUR TRIP INSIDE THE BORDER.

Apply glue here. Your items can be thick, thin, big, small, weird, interesting, funny, recycled, natural, unnatural, beautiful, ugly, bumpy, smooth, dead, living (no! just kidding!!! please, please, please don't do that!) Use just about anything that you think is awesome.

WiLdLife Bingo

Try to fill up one row (across, down or diagonal). You can do this in a race against someone else or set a goal for how long it will take you and race against the clock. It might look a little funny, but feel free to yell "BINGO" when you complete it. (Listen for other kids yelling BINGO too!)

WHEN YOU FIND ALL THE THINGS IN A BOX, PUT A BIG X ON THAT BOX.

1 Lizard	2 dolphins	4 tropical birds	1 school of fish

6 butterflies	1 manatee	3 sea stars	1 crab

Strange Things...

Find and photograph or sketch different, interesting or strange things you have found in Palm Beach (people, insects, plants, waterfalls, etc).

Go underwater, watch the waves, fish, etc., for as long as you can.
Write down your **observations**
(what did you see, hear feel… compare it to something).

WHAT DID YOU SEE?

WHAT DID YOU HEAR?

WHAT DID YOU FEEL?

WHAT DID YOU THINK?

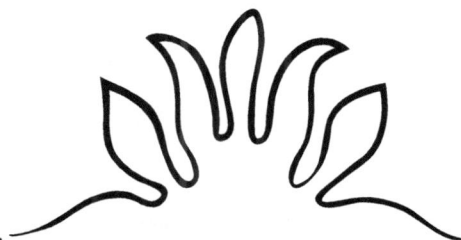

A BUGS EYE VIEW...

Lie on your back on the ground and look UP.

TAKE A PICTURE OR SKETCH WHAT YOU SEE FROM THIS DIFFERENT PERSPECTIVE.

Describe what you see in a couple of words.

...And a View from Above

Stand on the TALLEST place you can find
(TOP FLOOR OF YOUR HOTEL, A BALCONY, MOUNTAIN TOP, ETC.
JUST MAKE SURE IT IS A SAFE PLACE!)
Take a picture or sketch from this perspective. Describe what you see.

Tasty

Taste **4** new foods. What did you try? Where?
Photograph or sketch yourself eating one or more of the foods.

	FOOD	WHERE I TRIED IT	DID I LIKE IT? Yes	No
1st	_____	_____	◯	◯
2nd	_____	_____	◯	◯
3rd	_____	_____	◯	◯
4th	_____	_____	◯	◯

Here is a picture of me trying a new food!

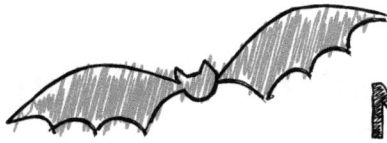

Nightlife!

What is the most memorable part about the night time in Palm Beach? What did you do or see at night? Take a picture or cut and glue pictures from brochures and postcards.

Describe what you see, hear, feel and smell.

Spot It

Record the BIGGEST or most interesting bugs you have seen in Palm Beach. Compare them to something else to describe the size.

The cockroach was bigger than my thumb!

THAT BUTTERFLY COULD HAVE EATEN A SANDWICH!

Wow that is OLD!

What is the oldest thing you have seen on Palm Beach?
Draw it or glue a picture. Describe it in one sentence.

PEOPLE ARE CRAZY!

What is the funniest or weirdest thing you have seen an adult do?
Describe it.

My *FAVORITE* Person
IN PALM BEACH

Take a picture or make a sketch of your favorite person at your hotel/restaurant/activity center.

Glue it here.

THIS IS _____

WE MET AT _____

I LIKED HIM/HER BECAUSE _____

_____

23

SIGN *Language*

Can you find a sign in another language? Record the words.
Take a picture or sketch it. What does the sign mean? Translate it.
(HINT: ASK SOMEONE AT YOUR HOTEL, RESTAURANT, ETC.)

Hello
(English)

Hola
(Spanish)

Kon-nichiwa
(Japanese)

Halo
(Indonesian)

Sawubona
(Zulu)

Hei
(Finish)

Aloha
(Hawaiian)

Dzien'dobry
(Polish)

Sholem
Aley Chem
(Yiddish)

Bonjour
(French)

Guten Tag
(German)

Ni hao
(Chinese Manderin)

GUESS WHO☺?

When you are on the beach, at the pool, on an airplane or at your hotel, find the back of someone's head. Without looking at their face, guess what it looks like. Draw or describe their face below and check if you're right.

This is for the Birds!

Take a picture (or sketch) a **tropical** bird.
Describe where you saw it and anything else you know about it.

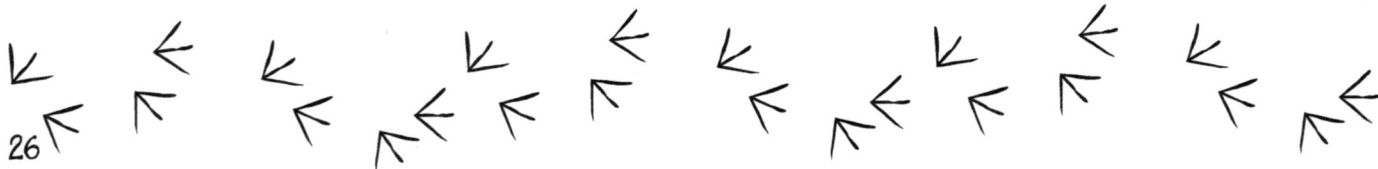

Nature Walk
Explore the nature in Palm Beach.
Take a picture or sketch the most interesting *Plant or Flower*.

OR YOU CAN GLUE A PETAL, LEAF OR BLOSSOM HERE.
DESCRIBE WHERE YOU FOUND IT AND ANYTHING ELSE YOU KNOW ABOUT IT.

ABC Vacation

Try to find something from your vacation — it can be anything — that starts with each letter of the alphabet!

A   B   C   D   E

F   G   H   I   J

K   L   M   N   O

P   Q   R   S   T

U   V   W   X   Y

Z

Baaaaad memories!

("UH, MY MOM FORGOT TO PACK MY UNDERWEAR." "THE WAITER DROPPED A PLATE OF SPAGHETTI ON MY HEAD!" "WE LIVED THROUGH A TYPHOON!")

What are some of the worst things that have happened on your trip?

Make list, take pictures, and/or glue something that reminds you of the worst things.

WEIRD things to do When you are bored...

Go to a crowded room/place of strangers and pretend you are a statue for 2 minutes. Count how many people notice you. Come up with 3 words or phrases to describe the experience. Take a picture of yourself or have someone take a picture of you while you are doing it.

Create your own Palm Beach drink. Come up with a tasty mix of tropical flavors, juices, fruit etc. Write down the ingredients and give it a cool tropical name.

NAME OF DRINK

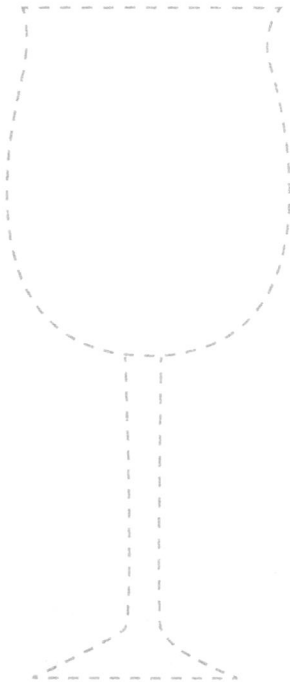

INGREDIENTS:

more weird things...

Find a famous or historical person that has been to Palm Beach or stayed in your hotel.
Hint: You can ask the people that work at the hotel, people in the town or read about the famous people in magazines or books about Palm Beach.

Dribble a few drops of ocean water here. Glue some sand and make a picture.

Collect straws, wrappers, paper coasters, mini umbrellas or other random things from the hotel or restaurants and glue them here...

another *weird* thing Vacation ORIGAMI
FIND THINGS TO MAKE.

Use a piece of scrap paper and fold it or shape it into something you have seen on your vacation like a shell, a starfish, a palm tree... anything! Just get creative. If you really have a problem, you can wad up a piece of paper and call it a coconut! *GLUE IT TO THIS PAGE.*

Palm Beach Word Scramble

Can you make at least 15 words using the letters in PALM BEACH, FL?
Answers in back...there are more than 95 words!!!

PALM BEACH, FL

"PALM BEACH ROCKS"

Design a t-shirt and a bumper sticker with a slogan or saying about your time in Palm Beach.

My Last hour in Palm Beach

The weather is:_____

It feels like: _____

I hear _____

I smell _____

I see _____

The thing I will miss the most about Palm Beach is...

The first thing I want to do when I get home is ...

The best part of Palm Beach was...

GOOD TIMES

Glue Pictures or Postcards from your favorite things or places on your trip.

GOOD TIMES

Glue Pictures or Postcards from your favorite things or places on your trip.

GOOD TIMES

Glue pictures or postcards from your favorite things or places on your trip.

GOOD TIMES

Glue pictures or Postcards from your favorite things or places on your trip.

GOOD TIMES

Glue Pictures or Postcards from your favorite things or Places on your trip.

GOOD TIMES

Glue Pictures or Postcards from your favorite things or places on your trip.

GOOD TIMES

Glue pictures or postcards from your favorite things or places on your trip.

Sample Pages

ABOUT THE AUTHOR

Jennie Tookoian is a teacher who received her B.A. from UC Berkeley and her M.A. in Education from Stanford University. She now teaches in California's Central Valley and specializes in teaching writing to kids of all ages. The activities in this book are pulled from the prompts she uses in her writing classes. They have been road-tested by her students and her own three children.

You can find more information at www.itsallgoodbooks.com

ABOUT THE ILLUSTRATOR

Elisabeth Markus is a graphic designer and illustrator living in Central California with her husband and two children. Working as a freelance designer for 20 years through her graphic design studio Early Moon Design, she also has a positive t-shirt website, www.gladditudes.com.

Palm Beach Word Scramble (page 33) word list: CAPABLE, APACHE, BEHALF, BLEACH, CHAPEL, PALACE, ALPHA, BEACH, BELCH, BLAME, CABLE, CAMEL, CHAMP, CHEAP, CLAMP, FABLE, FELLA, FLAME,18 LABEL, LLAMA, MAPLE, PEACH, PLACE, ABLE, ALEC, BACH, BALE, BALL, BALM, BEAM, BELL, BLAH, CAFE, CALF, CALL, CALM, CAME, CAMP, CAPE, CELL, CHAP, CHEF, CLAM, CLAP, EACH, FACE, FALL, FAME, FELL, FLAB, FLAP, FLEA, HALF, HALL, HEAL, HEAP, HELP, LACE, LAMB, LAME, LAMP, LEAF, LEAP, MACE, MALE, MALL, MEAL, PACE, PALE, PALM, PEAL, PLEA, ACE, AHA, ALL, ALP, APE, BAA, BAM, CAB, CAP, ELF, ELM, FAB, HAM, LAB, LAP, MAP, MEL, PEA, AM, BE, MA, ME, PA